Start a Lawn Business

Be Your Own Boss and Make a Great Living Mowing Grass

Mark Koger

Copyright © 2016 Mark Koger

All rights reserved.

ISBN: 1532838441
ISBN-13: 978-1532838446

DEDICATION

To Tonya Koger for always standing by my side.

Disclaimer

This book is intended for Informational purposes only.

Also, this book is relatively short. The information has been condensed to allow for quick reading and easy reference. Therefore it does not seek to answer every question someone may have regarding the lawn maintenance industry.

The author is not a lawyer or accountant. For matters involving the legalities of small business or the lawn maintenance industry please seek a professional lawyer. Any and all accounting or finance questions should be directed towards a professional accountant.

Information presented is strictly the opinion of the author. Please seek professional advice and/or counsel before acting upon any information in this book.

Earnings expressed or implied in this book should not be considered typical. Starting a business is risky and could result in financial loss.

Please investigate any and all products and services thoroughly before purchase or use.

No part of this publication shall be reproduced, transmitted, or sold in whole or in part in any form, without the prior written consent of the author. All trademarks and registered trademarks appearing in this book are the property of the respective owners.

By reading further you acknowledge and agree that the author is not responsible for the success or failure of your business especially as it relates to any information presented in this book.

CONTENTS

1. SHOULD I START MY OWN BUSINESS? 7
2. HOW I GOT MY FIRST FEW CLIENTS 11
3. 8 SIMPLE STEPS THAT GOT ME STARTED 16
4. HOW I BEGAN WITH VERY LITTLE MONEY 24
5. WHAT EQUIPMENT I STARTED OUT WITH 26
6. HOW I SET MY PRICES 30
7. THE IMPORTANCE OF COMPANY IMAGE 36
8. WHAT MY CLIENTS EXPECTED FROM ME 38
9. HOW I FOUND EMPLOYEES 43
10. HOW I HANDLED THE PAPERWORK.................45
11. HOW I HANDLED SUBCONTRACTORS 49
12. HOW TO MAKE THE LEAP FROM SMALL TO BIG 54
13. HOW I INCREASED MY SALES............................59
14. HOW I HANDLED COMPLAINTS 64
15. WHAT I DID WHEN IT RAINED 67
16. HOW I BEAT THE COMPETITION 69
17. HOW I GOT MORE MONEY OUT OF MY EXISTING CUSTOMERS 77
18. THE CUSTOMER I DIDN'T KNOW I HAD 82
19. HOW I HANDLED THE PRESSURE 84
20. WHY I WROTE THIS BOOK 86

1. SHOULD I START MY OWN BUSINESS?

I hated my job.

The money was fine. The work was not too bad. However, I didn't like the people I worked for. Let's just say that I believed I could do better for myself and my family.

I thought many times about starting my own small business. The problem was that I didn't know how to get started. And even if I could get started, I wasn't sure if I would make enough money to support my family. Also, I couldn't be certain that I would be any happier.

Looking back, I wish I hadn't hesitated. Starting my own lawn maintenance company was one of the best decisions of my life. I went from hating my job to loving my job.

I went from following orders to making my own schedule. I went from always worrying about money to always having money. I went from dreaming I was the boss to actually being the boss.

Sure, I made mistakes in the beginning. There are things I would go back and change if I could. **The number one thing I would do is get advice from someone who had been where I wanted to go.**

That is exactly why I've written this book.

I remember watching successful lawn maintenance companies and wondering how they grew their businesses. After many years and many mistakes my dream finally came true.

I started and developed a lawn maintenance company that was bringing in well over $1 million each year.

 What began with my wife and I grew to a company with over 30 employees. We had a fleet of trucks and trailers on the road. We eventually even had to rent a large commercial property with offices and a workshop.

Along the way I was able to stop mowing and start leading. I went where I wanted, when I wanted, and how I wanted.

Not to mention... I could finally afford the bass boat, four wheelers, and vacations I had always dreamed of.

The key to having a successful lawn maintenance company is found in a few basic principles. These principles are not hard. You just have to know what they are.

This book is a behind the scenes, insider's guide to starting and growing a successful lawn maintenance business.

In this book I explain exactly how I got started with just a few thousand dollars. I also explain my formula for making the leap from running one crew to running multiple crews. I teach how to bid and win commercial and residential accounts. I reveal how I found reliable employees and how I managed them. I also describe how I got more money from my existing customers.

Basically I share the most valuable guidelines for starting and growing a dream lawn maintenance business.

I am not a big reader. Therefore I have tried my best to condense all of the most valuable information into as few words as possible. I have also assumed that some readers may already have a company that they are trying to get to the next level. In that case, feel free to skip the first few chapters that explain the basics of how to get started.

This book is designed to reveal the inside information I always wished I had. It provides the clear plan of action I used to get my life and my company to the next level. In essence, this book exposes every tool I utilized to make more money, have a bigger impact, and improve my lifestyle.

There was a time in my life when I was scared to take the next step. I doubted myself and I didn't know how to get started.

Because I hesitated my life was miserable. Waiting around was the worst mistake I ever made.

It's true… being in business for myself was risky.

When I started, I wished I had a way to avoid the most common mistakes other lawn maintenance companies were making. That's exactly what this book is all about.

My desire is to equip others with the information they need to fulfill their dream of owning and operating a successful lawn maintenance business.

2. HOW I GOT MY FIRST FEW CLIENTS

My very first customer was someone I knew.

At the time I was still working for someone else. A friend of mine, who managed a local restaurant, gave me a call. She was having trouble finding a reliable lawn maintenance company. One day she said she wished I had a company of my own so she could hire me. This was just the encouragement I needed. She told me they could pay $500 a month. I told her I would do it.

The rest is history.

This restaurant was a well-known national brand (commercial account). So, the restaurant required certain credentials from me in order to start working for them.

I needed liability insurance, workers compensation insurance, commercial vehicle insurance, uniforms, and more. I know, it sounded like a lot to me too at the time. She explained to me that basically they wanted to know that they were dealing with someone who was trustworthy and responsible.

Unfortunately, I was not a professional company yet. **However, it was surprisingly simple to become one in very little time.** I'll reveal how I did that in the next chapter.

Once I had this first account it became easier to get more. I handed out business cards and told people to look into my work at the restaurant as a reference. My calling card was and always remained quality work, good communication, and a competitive price.

Before long I acquired several other commercial accounts. I also had a few homeowners who hired me (residential accounts).

Here are some basic principles I used to get more customers:

I told everyone I knew that I was in business.
I was very excited to have my own company. So I started telling people. It felt a little awkward at first. I didn't want to be too pushy. However, I found that most people were excited for me. After all, if I wasn't excited about my business then how could I expect anyone else to be?

I tapped into my social networks (friends) to get the word out.
I was not what some might call "well connected." I did however have some friends. They were big supporters for me during the first year. My family was also a great help. As I began to be vocal about my business I found out that I knew more people than I realized.

I walked into businesses and spoke with managers/owners about their lawn maintenance.
Sales is one of the hardest parts about owning your own business. This is especially true if you don't have any sales experience. It takes a lot of nerve to sell yourself and your company to complete strangers. Still, it is a necessary part of business. The good news is that people expect business owners to sell their products. Don't feel intimidated. Just put one foot in front of the other and tell them about your service.

If I noticed a yard that didn't look good, I asked for a chance to put in a bid.
Once I started my own business I began to see potential customers everywhere I went. If a lawn didn't look well-kept, then I would try to contact the person in charge and sell my services. Sometimes I was surprised at the people who took me up on my offer.

I offered a finder's fee to anyone who helped me get a new contract.

I created an incentive to get my friends and family to help me make contacts and sales. If they were able to help me get a new account then I would offer them 10% of the first month's contract price.

I was careful not to sell myself short (even though I was nervous).

I am not a pushy person. Many times I was tempted to shuffle my feet and down play my abilities when trying to make a sale. I had to learn that it was ok to be an expert in my field. There is a difference between bragging and confidence. I always tried my very best to display confidence.

I acted like a professional even though I didn't feel like one.

My whole life I have been a simple man. I consider myself just a regular guy. However, I learned that even though I never went to college or had much formal training, I was still a professional at my trade. This was my profession and I made every effort to be as skilled at possible.

Some jobs seemed too big but they usually turned out to be easier than I thought.
There were many occasions when I felt overwhelmed by a potential job. I almost turned many contracts down because they were bigger than what I was used to. In the end, I found that I was able to do far more than I gave myself credit for.

Throughout this book I will be sharing my personal experiences. I do this in hopes that you might identify with my experience and struggles. Most of all I pray it will give you the courage and inspiration to do things you never thought you could.

3. 8 SIMPLE STEPS THAT GOT ME STARTED

Starting a new business was very intimidating to me. I remember the feeling of anxiety quite well. There were so many questions. Sure, mowing grass was easy enough. However, the business side was scary. After all, I was just one man. The obstacles seemed overwhelming to me.

Fortunately it was not as hard as I thought it would be to start a professional company. That was great news because I couldn't stand working for my boss one more day.

8 simple steps I followed to get started:

1. I decided on a unique company name.
2. I filed the appropriate paperwork with my state.
3. I purchased liability and workers compensation insurance.
4. I purchased commercial vehicle insurance.
5. I opened a separate business checking account.
6. I got shirts/uniforms made with a simple logo.
7. I had business cards made.
8. I created a basic contract for my customers to sign.

Now let me explain these steps a little further.

STEP 1: I decided on a unique name.

This was an exciting part of the business creation process. I knew that people should be able to tell what my company did just by hearing the name. The hardest part was finding something unique.

To help with this step I went to my state's "Division of Corporations" web site. Try using an internet search engine (like Google or Bing) to find your state's equivalent. My state allowed me to easily search their records. I compared the name I wanted my company to have to names that already existed.

After searching a few options I settled on a name that was easy to pronounce and that fit my personality. I also made sure that the name clearly communicated what my company did (i.e. lawn maintenance/landscaping).

STEP 2: I filed the appropriate paperwork with my state.

There are several options for people to follow to make their company a legitimate legal business. My company was incorporated. Some people choose LLC. Your state's Division of Corporations web site should be able to direct you through this process. Expect to pay a fee to file the paperwork. You may also choose to consult a lawyer or tax accountant (for an additional fee of course). This step can seem intimidating but it is simpler than most people think.

PRO TIP: After you file your paperwork, some dishonest companies may send you a letter in the mail asking for more money to file additional paperwork. Do your research to make sure this is not a scam. These companies often pose as fake governmental agencies.

STEP 3: I purchased liability and workers compensation insurance.

Some lawn maintenance providers choose to bypass this step. However, keep in mind that skipping this step places a company at unnecessary risk. Lawn maintenance can easily cause unintended property damage or physical harm. Also, large commercial accounts (the kind I was mostly involved with) will not hire you without the proper proof of insurance.

Contact the insurance companies of your choice and explain that you are starting a lawn maintenance business. They will be able to assist you with what you will need.

Many times your customers will tell you exactly what dollar amount of insurance they require. Usually it was one to three million dollars in coverage. To be clear, this did not mean that I paid one million dollars. It meant that the insurance company would pay up to that amount if there was an accident. This was not as expensive as it sounded. Don't be intimidated.

> **PRO TIP:** When I contacted commercial customers I would ask them several questions. If they were interested in a bid I would ask what liability insurance they required. This made it appear that I knew what I was doing.

STEP 4: I purchased commercial vehicle insurance.

This can be done with the previous step. Again, most commercial accounts will require this type of coverage before a company can begin work. Having it in place gave my company an image of professionalism and experience.

STEP 5: I opened a separate business checking account.

Most of my customers expected to pay by writing a check to a professional company and not to me as an individual. Therefore, I would need a checking account in my business's name. This step also helped to keep my business money and personal money from running together. My bank was an important partner in the long term success of my company.

To open the bank account I simply walked into the bank and told them that I was starting a new business and wanted to open a business checking account. They helped answer my questions and the process was fairly straight forward. I started by using the bank that held my personal account.

STEP 6: I had shirts/uniforms made with a simple logo.

Customers expect lawn maintenance workers to wear a basic uniform with a company logo. These uniforms can consist of a company shirt with jeans or solid colored work pants.

The company logo does not need to be fancy. Most t-shirt printing companies will be able to design something basic. Make sure the design suits the image you want your company to project. It should be simple, easy to read, and appealing. It also helps if the logo is different than your competitors.

Don't get bogged down during this step. Decide on a simple design and color scheme and move on.

> **PRO TIP:** In my experience local t-shirt shops are often less expensive than buying online. Professional uniform providers usually cost more but can be an option as your company grows.

STEP 7: I had business cards made.

Business cards are essential. These can sometimes be purchased at the same place your t-shirts are made. Online providers like Vistaprint.com are also a good option for business cards and other printed marketing materials. There are hundreds of marketing materials you could buy but I found business cards to work the best. Bear in mind that brochures, signs, and giveaways do not always create more sales. Keep it simple. Later I will reveal how my company grew with almost no advertising.

STEP 8: I created a basic contract.

I always tried to get each customer to agree to sign a 12 month contract before I started service. This contract detailed the specifics of what my company would provide the customer. This was essential when servicing business accounts like restaurants, doctor's offices, and shopping malls.

IT INCLUDED:

- How often I would mow?
- Would I keep the hedges trimmed?
- Would I control the weeds?
- Would I edge the driveway?
- Would I provide annual flowers?
- What would I charge per month?
- How would my customers pay?

Every contract is different. A lawyer could be helpful to make sure the wording is right. You might consider searching the internet for sample contracts to use as reference.

PRO TIP: Some customers will not want to agree to a 12 month contract. I offered a discount if they signed up for one. In the slow growing season, a 12 month contract ensured that I still had some money coming in.

4. HOW I BEGAN WITH VERY LITTLE MONEY

Lawn maintenance equipment is very costly. When starting out, this can be a major upfront expense. However, it should not hinder anyone from the dream of owning their own lawn maintenance business.

Here are the exact steps I took to get the basic equipment I needed:

- I approached a few family members about the possibility of getting a small loan. I borrowed $3,000.
- I already had a pickup truck that would work for the time being.
- I purchased a smaller trailer just large enough to get me by.

- I went to the local lawn equipment store and purchased all used professional equipment.
- I used what tools I already had or could borrow.
- See WHAT EQUIPMENT I GOT STARTED WITH

The first few months were tight because everything was billed 30 days out. That means that I did the work for a whole month without having any income. I'll explain more about that in the HOW I HANDLED THE PAPERWORK section of this book.

My wife and I toughed it out while living as thrifty as possible. Eventually the checks started coming in from my customers. I will admit the first few months were scary but well worth the risk.

PRO TIP: Don't ask for special favors at the lawn equipment shop right away. I made sure to always pay my bills on time. After they got to know me they were usually willing to work out a payment plan for me when I was in a pinch.

5. WHAT EQUIPMENT I STARTED OUT WITH

There are many places a person can go to find lawn equipment.

First, I located a commercial lawn equipment dealer in my area. These shops may cost a little more than the big box stores but their equipment will typically work better and last longer. Plus, these shops serviced my equipment quickly when I needed repairs.

> **PRO TIP:** I developed a good working relationship with the lawn equipment shop manager and its owner. These people tended to have valuable information about industry trends. They also offered money saving advice.

Commercial lawn equipment shops often carry used equipment. Yes, this can be risky. However, purchasing used equipment allowed me to get started with a low upfront investment. County auctions may also have well maintained used equipment.

The Essential Tools:

- **Pickup Truck**
    - Any full-size pickup (Ford F150, Chevy 1500, etc.) will work for basic lawn maintenance.
    - I eventually started using ¾ ton pickups (Ford F250, Chevy 2500, etc.).

- **Trailer 12'-16'**
    - These trailers are usually painted black with a gate on the back that swings down turning into a ramp. They may have one or two tires per side depending on size.
    - I got started with a small used trailer until I could afford something larger.

- **Lawn Mower**
    - In most cases I needed a zero turn lawn mower.
    - There are riding and stand up varieties available.

- **String Trimmer**
    - Some people call these weed eaters or line trimmers.
    - Make sure to get a straight shaft trimmer.
    - They cost a bit more but will save your back in the long run.
- **Stick Edger**
    - A stick edger is shaped similar to a string trimmer.
    - It keeps a clean edge between the grass and hard surfaces as well as plant beds.
- **Hedge Trimmers**
    - A gas powered version works best.
    - These come in long and short varieties.
    - Buy whatever you can afford to get you started.
- **Blower**
    - A backpack blower is ideal for quick clean up after mowing.
    - To get started I used a commercial hand held blower.

Other Essential Equipment:

- 5 Gallon Gas Can (for mower)
- 2 Gallon Gas Can (for two cycle mixed gas)
- Two-Cycle Oil
- Replacement Edger Blades
- Edger Adjustment Tool
- Extra Line for String Trimmer
- Rake
- Shovel
- Eye Protection
- Hearing Protection

Optional Tools:

- Chainsaw
- Backpack Sprayer
- Hand Held Pruners (Snips)
- Loppers
- Gloves
- Tarp
- Trash Can

6. HOW I SET MY PRICES

Many factors influenced the prices I charged. These often included fuel costs, quality of services provided, and number of competitors.

Every city is different.

When the economy was doing well, prices tended to rise. When the economy was bad, prices tended to fall.

However, in almost every case I priced a job based on a per hour rate. Larger, more complex landscapes took more time. Therefore I charged more money.

First I would estimate how many "man hours" it might take to complete the required work. Say for example that a job would take three workers, two hours to complete. Then that would equal six "man hours" (3 x 2 = 6).

Afterward, I would apply my per hour rate times six. If my per hour rate was $30 then that would be 6 x $30 = $180.

That's what I would charge, $180 per mow. Billing monthly that would be $720 (4 weeks x $180).

Everyone's per hour rate will be different. This rate had to cover all of my expenses and also leave some room for profit.

> **PRO TIP:** Taking time to talk with other landscape professionals would sometimes reveal what the standard pricing for a certain job should be.

Residential Accounts

> **PRO TIP:** Some residential neighborhoods had a standard expectation regarding the rates they were willing to pay. In the beginning I even tried calling a few local competitors and asked what they might charge to mow my own lawn. This helped me know what I should charge.

Neighbors usually talk to one another. If one house pays $90 per month and is happy with their service they will usually tell their friends.

Sometimes a customer would expect a lower price than I thought was reasonable. However, if I could get several more accounts very close to one another then it made the prospect more profitable. This was due to the fact that I wasn't wasting time or gas traveling from yard to yard.

> **PRO TIP:** I would often agree to a somewhat low paying residential account. Then I would knock on every door in the neighborhood and try to get more business. This turned one small account into a half day's work.

Speed is a big factor when it comes to making more money in lawn maintenance. As the old saying goes, "time is money." People who are not used to mowing every day will be somewhat slow in the beginning.

With experience comes speed.

Keep in mind that I also had to maintain a high level of quality. As I repeatedly mowed the same places I was able to get faster.

The faster I was, the more money I made in a day.

Commercial Accounts

Commercial jobs (mowing businesses) were sometimes more difficult to price than residential jobs. As mentioned, residential jobs are pretty standard when it comes to pricing.

Don't let commercial jobs intimidate you.

I constantly had to remind myself not to be afraid of big jobs. In fact, every time I pushed myself I was glad I did. When I turned big jobs down…I always regretted it.

Sometimes I wasn't sure how many man hours a property might take to complete. This was especially true for large properties. In these cases I would divide the landscape into smaller parts in my mind. I would come up with a price for each small component and then add them all together to get the final price. This helped make the bidding process more manageable.

The more experience I got the better I became at bidding properties.

> **PRO TIP:** Sometimes your subcontractors (like pest control companies) may be willing to reveal what they know other landscape companies are charging for services.

The Secret Weapon I Used to Set My Prices

My greatest advantage would come when I could find out what the customer was already paying for their lawn services. Most times I would just come out and ask, "**Would you mind sharing how much you currently pay per month for your lawn maintenance**?"

I always had to be careful because I did not want to appear rude.

When bidding a commercial account, it was sometimes helpful to try to locate a maintenance person on the property. I might even ask to speak to the head maintenance person.

This often yielded invaluable information for me. Maintenance professionals are often more willing to discuss prices and expectations. I usually tried to make some kind of small talk. If they liked me, then I would have a better chance of landing the account.

I developed some sincere friendships using this process. These friendships helped to rapidly grow my business. When my friends got promoted or moved to a new company...they often took me with them.

PRO TIP: Utilize covert surveillance. Sometimes I was totally stumped and couldn't decide what to charge for a property. So I would wait and watch the current lawn maintenance provider mow the property. However long it took them was about how long it should take me. Then I would apply my hourly rate based on that information.

7. THE IMPORTANCE OF COMPANY IMAGE

In the beginning, I did whatever I had to do to get by. My truck wasn't the newest. My equipment wasn't the best. I didn't have a web site or fancy marketing materials. I was a man with a humble lawn maintenance business.

However, as I grew I made sure to invest in my company. Eventually I was able to purchase a gently used pickup truck that was clean and presentable. This was the truck I used to visit customers and bid new projects.

> **PRO TIP:** I was always careful not to over dress when meeting with customers. I typically wore jeans and a polo type shirt with my company logo. Not too fancy, not too casual.

I also made sure that my trucks were all the same color. White was usually easy enough to find and appeared clean. I also had each truck lettered with vinyl decals that included my company name, logo, and phone number. We cleaned the vehicles no less than once a week. Sometimes we cleaned them more often.

My employees were always in some type of uniform. This was occasionally a challenge. A simple logoed shirt with jeans or solid colored pants worked fine for me. I didn't allow anyone to wear sleeveless shirts or ripped shirts. I also made sure they did not go shirtless at any time.

8. WHAT MY CLIENTS EXPECTED FROM ME

Every client was different. Therefore, good communication was very important when first starting a new account. There were, however, a few basic things that almost every customer expected. Some of this information is quite basic. Nevertheless, I was sometimes surprised at the mistakes I saw other businesses make over my 30 years of experience.

Mowing
- During growing season grass should be mowed every week.
- The growing season is different for every region.
- Typically the growing season lasts from spring to fall.

- Different species of grass should be mowed at different heights.
- If you cut certain grasses too short (sometimes called scalping) you risk causing disease and weeds.
- It is not acceptable to leave any areas of grass not mowed (even very small spots).
- Be careful that you do not leave tire ruts from your heavy lawn mower.
- Mow in straight lines as much as possible.

String Trimming

- I used this tool to cut the grass in areas that the mower could not get to.
- I trimmed around plant beds, mail boxes, poles, and other small areas.
- Again, it was never acceptable to leave small blades of grass sticking up.
- I was always careful not to damage any property (buildings, vehicles, toys, hoses, etc.).

Edging

- During growing season I edged the sidewalks, curbs and driveways every week.
- The planting beds were edged once every other week.

Blowing

- My customers expected their driveways, porches, patios, and roadsides to be blown clean after every service.
- This was true even if I did not cause the mess.
- All hardscape areas were blown clean with a powerful backpack blower.
- Before we left a property we made sure that there was no grass, dirt, or debris lying on the hardscapes.

Hedge Trimming

- Hedges of different varieties grow at different rates during different times of the year.
- I usually trimmed hedges once a month.

- I divided large properties into sections and did a little each week.
- The key was to keep them looking well kept at all times.
- It was not acceptable to have long stems poking out all over the hedge.
- The hedges were expected to be as perfectly level and smooth as possible.
- It was also important to keep the back of the hedges trimmed away from structures even if no one would notice for a while.
- My customers expected the clippings to be picked up after trimming.
- Hedge trimming was not included in every contract.

Weeding

- Weed control was only done on an as needed basis.
- Some weeds can be easily and quickly pulled by hand.
- Other types of weeds require a non-selective herbicide spray (weed killer).
- Be aware that many states have laws regulating the application of any herbicide. This even includes very small businesses.
- The state in which I operated in required that

- we send a few employees once a year to be licensed.
- This was a hassle, but so was the fine they imposed for violation of their rule.
- I usually purchased large containers of herbicide and applied it with a backpack sprayer.
- Anyone applying chemicals of any kind should follow all manufacturers' instructions at all times.
- I was always careful not to let any herbicide get on the grass or plants.
- Weed control was not included in every contract.

Keep in mind that any contract can be customized to provide any variety of the services mentioned above. This is simply a list of common expectations my clients had. Good communication is the key to happy customers. One person's weed is another person's prized flower.

9. HOW I FOUND EMPLOYEES

When I first started out I only had a few accounts. The work was not too overwhelming but neither was the income. Therefore I did most of the work myself. My wife would sometimes mow while I did the harder leg work. Eventually, I was able to land a few more jobs. After a short time of working alone I began needing employees. Here are the methods I used to find good workers.

- Sometimes I found a family member or neighbor looking for employment.
- I asked around at the local mower shop to see if they knew of any experienced workers looking for employment.
- I sometimes asked if I could post a flyer stating that I was hiring.
- I asked current employees if they could recommend anyone.

- Occasionally I had people approach me looking for employment. I asked them fill out a short application and kept it on file for later.
- I offered a referral program. If a person helped me find and secure a good worker they would receive a modest gift card. This was usually given only if the new employee lasted past the 90 day mark.
- When I needed employees it helped to be vocal about my needs. I got the word out amongst my social circle (church, neighborhood, cookouts, etc.).
- Usually, I tried to hire workers with some experience. I considered hiring those with no experience during the slow season to allow time for training them.
- During summer there was less time to train.

Keep in mind that lawn maintenance is a very physically demanding line of work. Some people will not be up to the challenge. Others will work too slowly. Some will need a lot of training. Still others may not be reliable.

I kept all of these things in consideration before I agreed to hire any employee. **At the end of the day an employee with the right attitude goes a long way.** It was often worth the extra effort to train or condition an employee who demonstrated values, integrity, and strong work ethic.

10. HOW I HANDLED THE PAPERWORK

I am not an office kind of person. Billing, finance, and employee records made me cringe. Thankfully my wife was willing to help with these tasks in the beginning. Later, I was able to hire employees to handle these important duties. Here are the procedures we used.

Billing

Customers were sent a monthly invoice (bill). The invoice included the service provided and the cost. It also included a due date, invoice number, and return address. Very basic invoice pads can be purchased from most office supply stores.

Invoices were sent to each customer once a month on a regular schedule. If I was sloppy with this step then it delayed my payments – NOT GOOD!

Computer software was used to keep track of all customers, addresses, and prices. Spreadsheet software like Microsoft Excel was an inexpensive option for me when just starting out.

Some smaller customers desired to pay me in person with cash. However, most customers wanted to pay with a check in the mail.

As the money came in I needed a system to verify which customers had paid and which had not. A simple check list works just fine. The important thing is to keep very good records. You must be sure who has paid and who has not. It is not acceptable to accuse your customers of not paying just because you made an invoicing mistake.

Finance

It was sometimes tempting to manage everything in cash and skip the steps below. However, I had to keep in mind that to grow my company I needed to handle my money in a professional manner.

After a few months we started using a software program called Quickbooks Pro. This program was a few hundred dollars but well worth the expense. It gave my business a professional edge and helped to manage all of my money.

Part of the finance job duties included keeping track of every receipt. This meant that all expenses (gas, oil, parts, equipment, etc.) need a physical receipt to be kept and filed. The receipts were then entered into the software program as an expense.

These records were later compared with monthly bank statements by a process called reconciling. The entire billing process could be handled using the software program.

Once my revenue grew to hundreds of thousands of dollars I began to realize just how necessary this type of software was. Thankfully, there was affordable training available through books, seminars, and internet videos.

There were also book keepers who I could have hired to handle this task for me.

Employee Records

We required every employee to fill out an application before they were hired. We also collected proof of identification. Each employee's records were kept in their own file and locked for safety.

In the early stages we calculated state payroll taxes using Quickbooks Pro. Later we hired a payroll company to handle this task for us. We were also able to provide our employees insurance benefits through this payroll company.

The payroll company was an extra expense but one we felt was well worth it. Every payroll company is different but we were always happy with our experience.

11. HOW I HANDLED SUBCONTRACTORS

Many times throughout my business experience I ran into customers who wanted services that I could not provide. Sometimes I did not have the right license, equipment, or knowledge. However, my customers viewed me as a one stop shop. Thankfully there were always people who I could pay to do the work for me. These were called subcontractors.

I commonly used subcontractors for pest and fertilizer treatment, irrigation, landscaping, tractor work, tree trimming, mulching, and even lawn maintenance.

I made it clear that these companies worked for me. My name was attached to every job they did so it needed to be done right. I also made sure they would travel wherever I needed them. Sometimes this meant driving an hour or more to get to the project.

Fertilizer and Pest Company

There are many laws that regulate who can apply certain chemicals to landscapes. Due to these laws I regularly hired a pest control company to treat my customer's lawns for me. Usually this service was included in the price of the contract with my customers. Therefore I would bill the customer at one time for everything. My subcontractors would later get paid by me.

It was important to hire a very reputable company who would stand behind their work. Occasionally mistakes did happen. When they did I would hold the pest company accountable to fix the problem.

Sometimes these companies can be quite expensive. The goal is to find a good company who you can have a lasting relationship with.

I usually tried asking at the local mower shop or fertilizer supply shop who they might recommend.

PRO TIP: I eventually found a pest control contractor who was just starting a new business of his own. He was trying to make a name for himself. Therefore he was willing to do quality work for much less than I was currently paying. Today we are best friends.

Suppliers

In addition to subcontractors I also had many other companies who were vital to my businesses success. These suppliers provided me with equipment, materials, and services. Each one was essential to helping my business thrive.

Over the years I was able to develop great relationships with these suppliers. Ultimately I expected what my customers expected: a fair price, reliability, speed, and exceptional customer service. The more I did business with these suppliers the more they were willing to go out of their way to help me succeed.

Here is a list of suppliers I often needed:

- Mulch Companies
- Annual Flower Nurseries
- Landscape Nurseries
- Payroll Companies
- Fertilizer Suppliers
- Mower Shops
- Print Shops
- Insurance Companies
- Mechanics
- Truck Dealerships
- Gas Stations
- Dumps/Landfills
- Sod Suppliers
- Rock Suppliers
- Paver Companies

The good news is that I did not need to have relationships with all of these companies before I could start my business. These relationships were formed over many years.

> **PRO TIP:** Hardware stores can be a great one stop shop for many landscape supplies. When my business was smaller this worked fine for me. However, I found that I saved a lot of money by purchasing bulk materials from professional wholesale providers.

I will discuss a few other subcontractors in another chapter.

12. HOW TO MAKE THE LEAP FROM SMALL TO BIG

Over the years I met a lot of guys who were operating their business with one truck and one trailer. They made decent money and got to make their own schedules. This is a relatively simple business to run for anyone who is willing to get out there and mow every day.

However, at some point most people desire to grow their business and grow their income. A larger business with multiple crews on the road provides a measure of security. There were times when I was hurt or sick. Fortunately my business still made money even when I couldn't physically work. Another benefit of growing your business is that you eventually get to make the switch from mower to manager.

The big question is, how do you make the leap from small to big?

It requires a sizable investment to purchase all of the equipment for another crew. Most people who are making a living with just one crew are busy working long hours during the growing season. Taking on a few extra yards here and there will not pay enough to hire even one full time worker.

As overwhelming as all of this seems, it's really not impossible. Keep these things in mind.

How to Handle More Employees

- Employees do not cost, they earn.
- Without more employees I struggled to grow.
- There came a point when I couldn't do it all myself.
- I got used to the idea of having and managing employees.
- Lawn maintenance is a labor intensive business.
- On the flip side, I did not hire more employees than I actually needed.
- For tips on finding more workers refer to HOW I FOUND EMPLOYEES

How to Afford the Equipment

- Buy used.
- I didn't always need the newest truck and trailer.
- I understood that a small investment now would pay off in the long run.

How to Get More Work for Your New Crew

- I used the slow growing season to focus on sales.
- I remembered that more crews on the road increased my visibility.
- More employees meant I could now bid larger, more profitable jobs.
- Refer to HOW I INCREASED MY SALES

How I Made Sure the Crews Were Doing Their Job

- I was always training one of my current employees to take over my new crew when the time came.
- This was someone I trusted and who knew my company standards and values.
- I made the crew leader a higher paid, prestigious position that other employees aspired to be promoted to.
- A growing company sent the message to employees that there would be opportunities for advancement.
- GPS tracking was a great way to keep everyone in check.
- This also allowed me to increase my productivity with routes.
- I or someone I trusted periodically inspected the work being done at every job site (usually every week).

PRO TIP: Every new crew began the exact same way my first crew did. All I had to do was duplicate the same principles. In my experience, it was almost always worth the risk and investment.

13. HOW I INCREASED MY SALES

I remember when I landed my first big commercial account. I knew that I could live on that income alone and be comfortable. However, my desire was to grow a business that could provide for me for the rest of my life. Therefore, I needed more customers.

I learned an important lesson early on. **In order to grow I had to get off of the mower and focus on sales and management.** In the long run I had to invest in employees who could also manage and sell.

> **PRO TIP:** When hiring top level employees it is essential to ask them to sign a non-compete agreement. This is standard industry procedure and keeps them from starting their own business and stealing your customers.

I do not consider myself a good salesperson. I have never studied sales techniques or went to business school. However, I learned one thing that is essential to business success. **I had to get out and meet people.**

I went everywhere I could, meeting people and telling them about my business. I joined the chamber of commerce, apartment associations, and trade groups. I went to HOA meetings, apartment association meetings, county and public works meetings. For every small commercial job I landed I would try to find their corporate office and visit. That visit would often lead to more accounts. Usually I didn't have to push sales very hard. I simply introduced myself, smiled, and thanked them for the opportunity to meet.

> **PRO TIP:** Every big account I ever had was due to a positive relationship that I developed with someone.

Visiting Local Businesses

In the beginning, I began visiting businesses similar to the ones I already had accounts with. I asked to meet the manager briefly and gave them my card. I asked if they were accepting bids on their lawn maintenance contract.

Many said no - some said yes.

If they said no, then I would go back again in a few weeks. I would visit at least three times or more before giving up.

If they said yes then I drove or walked around the property and made a note of how much I thought I could reasonably charge (see HOW I SET MY PRICES).

I would often try to locate the head maintenance worker and introduce myself to him/her.

I would inform them that I was going to be bidding the property. Then I would ask if there were any current problems that I should know about.

> **PRO TIP:** If there were any landscape issues then I took the opportunity to demonstrate my expertise by offering free advice. My goal was to demonstrate that I was an easy person to work with and that I could be an asset.

This of course applies mainly to commercial accounts.

Cold Calling

I put my wife and adult daughter to work making calls to different types of businesses. In this way we developed a specialty for certain types of properties.

She would get out the phone book and call everyone on the list. Then she would ask if they were accepting bids for their lawn maintenance.

Many said no - some said yes.

If they said yes, we would repeat the steps mentioned above.

Sometimes she would also fax or email marketing materials to these potential customers.

Referrals

An overwhelming amount of my company's growth came from referrals. We worked hard to provide great customer service.

I eventually hired my daughter full time to make sure that our clients were happy.

I on the other hand developed a great working relationship with the maintenance professionals.

Whatever they needed, we got it done. If we made a mistake, we fixed it right away. If they needed us to work under a certain budget, we did.

As a result, when their colleagues asked if they knew of any good lawn maintenance companies they gave out our number. This resulted in explosive growth.

14. HOW I HANDLED COMPLAINTS

The worst part about being in business was dealing with complaints. Some people would complain about the hedges being too short. Others would complain that they were too tall.

Still other people called claiming that I damaged their property or their vehicle. Some complained about how my employees behaved.

No matter how silly the complaint was, I treated each one as though it were important.

My customers were my pay check. They kept food on my table and the tables of all of my employees. If they weren't happy then I did everything I could to address the problem as quickly as possible.

Here are some tips for handling complaints:

- I didn't let my anger show even if I was being yelled at.
- I was polite no matter what.
- A smile and humble attitude can quickly diffuse an angry customer.
- "Yes sir" went a long way.
- I provided an immediate solution to the complaint.
- My customers appreciated decisive action.
- The customer was always right (almost).

My rule of thumb for handling complaints was - Be nice and fix it.

Following this simple formula allowed my company to skyrocket past the competition. My customers respected and trusted me. Therefore they recommended me to their friends.

In the end I found that is all most people want. They desire a lawn maintenance company who can be trusted to do their job right.

PRO TIP: Occasionally, some people would claim that my company caused hundreds of dollars of damage to a vehicle or home. In those cases, I thoroughly investigated the accusations. If my company could have reasonably caused the damage, I asked the person to get a few quotes to fix the damage. I would then write a check directly to the repair company. After explaining these procedures, most people would just say to forget the whole matter. Turns out all they wanted was some quick cash.

15. WHAT I DID WHEN IT RAINED

I can't tell you how many times I lost money by listening to a false weather report. Over the years I learned not to trust them. That being said, bad weather does happen.

Despite weather, my customers expected to have their lawns looking good all of the time. That's what they were paying me for. However, Mother Nature sometimes made that difficult. This was especially true during the busy growing season when rain was most likely.

Here is what I did when it rained.

- Most times I found that work could be performed in light rain with little hindrance.

- If the rain was heavy I would rest in the truck until it stopped.
- My work had to continue rain or shine.
- The rain caused the grass to be soggy and harder to cut.
- We had to be very careful not to cause large tire ruts in the lawn.
- Blowing off the hardscape areas also took a lot longer when things were wet.
- We did not work if it was dangerous (lightning, tornados, high winds, etc.).
- When an area of grass was too wet to mow I would use a string trimmer.

Communication with our customers was always essential. If we had a slowdown in production we would contact our customers and explain the situation to them. Most customers were very understanding.

It was only when I failed to communicate about rain delays that my customers complained regarding them.

16. HOW I BEAT THE COMPETITION

One day I submitted a proposal to maintain the landscaping at a large apartment complex. I knew the maintenance manager who was also in charge of several other apartment complexes in the area. We already had some accounts with the company and I figured we had a good chance to get this one as well. A couple of days later he called me back and mentioned that another company had undercut my price significantly. After a few tweaks to the contract I was able to land the account.

This was an ongoing battle in the lawn maintenance business. Competition will never go away. There will always be someone somewhere who is willing to do what you do for less money. As I've already said, sometimes I had to agree to a lower price than I wanted. However, there came times when I couldn't just drop my prices to beat the competition.

So I found a way to make my services more desirable.

Customer service was my number one weapon.

It's true, almost anyone with a mower can make grass short. But that's not what the lawn maintenance business is all about.

I built a reputation as a person who could be trusted to help my customers have a beautiful, problem free, landscape for the long term. My customers counted on me to be a problem solver. When I did this right my business grew.

Here are a few things I did to set myself apart from the competition.

1. I Was an Expert

To be clear, I never went to college. I did not know the scientific names of plants. I was not familiar with the latest and greatest information coming out of the horticultural industry. Thankfully, I did not need to be.

What I did need to know were the most common problems that my customers would encounter. I researched these problems and found the best solutions. As time went by I began to be able to answer customer's questions quite easily.

Every area of the country has problems that are specific to that region.

I would pay attention to only those problems that applied to my area of the country. Then I would find solutions to them.

For example, a customer might show me a dying plant and ask what's wrong.

It could be heat, cold, too dry, too wet, disease, insects, wrong soil, drainage, irrigation, too much shade, too much sun, too much mulch, not enough mulch, harmful chemicals, trampled, eaten, etc.

Most times identifying the problem just took common sense.

However sometimes I was stumped.

When this happened I would say something like, "I think I know the problem but just to be sure I need to take a sample to be analyzed."

This would give me some time to get to the bottom of the problem.

Here are a few things I did to find the solution.

- I searched the internet.
- I looked it up in a book.
- I took a sample to the local lawn chemical/fertilizer supply store.
- I would ask my pest control subcontractor to take a look for me.
- I might also take a soil sample to be analyzed.

The important thing was to provide a solution to the problem as quickly as possible. This could also be an opportunity to upsell another one of your services (irrigation, pest control, new landscaping).

If the area was too dry, I would sell an irrigation system. If the problem was pests, I would sell a chemical treatment. Occasionally plants get old just like people. In that case, I would sell a new landscape installation.

2. I Went Above and Beyond Expectations

Sometimes just getting the job done is challenging. After all, lawn maintenance is hot, back breaking, exhaustive work. That's why many lawn maintenance businesses seem to do as little as possible. That's also why I was able to beat the competition.

Just a little extra effort goes a long way. And the best part is that all I had to do was a little above what others were doing.

Here are just a few of the things I did.

- I gave my best customers a gift at Christmas (usually a fresh cut Christmas tree).
- I randomly gave gift cards to property managers.
- I would place some nicely potted plants near the front door.
- I took customers out to lunch.
- I would write hand written letters thanking them for their business.
- I would gift sports tickets to decision makers in large companies.
- I also took them golfing.
- We would bring newspapers to their doorstep.
- We gave courtesy calls from the office when we were running late.
- We kept up our equipment, trucks, and employee's appearance.

Before we left a property after mowing we would ask ourselves, what's something extra we could do that would make a big impact?

3. I Was Kind

My philosophy was, if people liked me they would hire me. I always made sure to have a smile on my face. To be honest, many times I was hot, exhausted, and sore. I did not feel like smiling but I did it anyway. At least, I did when talking to customers.

I listened with concern to my customer's needs and problems. Sometimes I was frustrated with my customers. They were often unreasonable, irritable, and overdramatic. But I listened and helped them anyway. And I did it with a smile.

> **PRO TIP:** I was the face of my company. I knew that at the end of the day people expected me to see to it that their landscaping was done and done right. I did not have to physically do all of the work. But I was responsible for all of the work.

4. I Kept My Prices Competitive in Creative Ways

There are many niche markets in the lawn maintenance business. There are high end jobs, low end jobs, specialty jobs, eco-friendly jobs, and everything in between. However, very few customers want to pay more than they think they should. Therefore, I had to get creative with my pricing strategy.

Occasionally a customer would ask me to do a job for a price that was too low for me to make a profit. Sometimes I would take the job anyway. But only if I thought the account would bring in good leads or create a good relationship with an important decision maker. After a year of providing outstanding service I would raise my price.

Sometimes I would include an add-on service at my cost. For example many of my customers wanted mulch installed annually. During the growing season I was too busy to worry about installing mulch. So, I would agree to install the mulch at cost but only during the slower growing months.

Other times I would offer to inspect a customer's irrigation system for free in their contract. However, any repairs or parts would be an extra charge.

Sometimes I included other small services for free or at my cost in order to up sell another service later.

In the end, I believed in my company. I felt we provided a top notch service at a great price. And that is what I sold to my customers. I didn't always beat the competition but I did continually grow my company every year.

17. HOW I GOT MORE MONEY OUT OF MY EXISTING CUSTOMERS

There is a busy season and a slow season in lawn maintenance. When the grass was growing it was a full time job to keep it cut. However, the cooler months included a lot of down time. This was a great opportunity to take a much deserved rest. However, it was also a great occasion to use my labor force to make more money. Here is a list of service I marketed and sold to my existing customers.

Annual Flowers

- Many commercial clients (and even some residential ones) loved the idea of having bright beautiful flowers adorning their properties.
- I would charge for each flower when installing the annuals.

- Usually this was about double what I paid per flower.
- Large quantities of these types of flowers, planted in rows, worked best.
- After a few jobs it became easier to estimate how many flowers would be needed.
- The job required any existing old flowers to be removed from the plant bed.
- The area was then treated with fertilizer and fungicide.
- After tilling the ground, the new plants were able to be planted at a very quick pace.
- All I had to do was bury the roots and make sure the rows were straight.
- I also made sure that the irrigation system was set to water these flowers adequately.

Mulch

- First I researched the benefits of mulch on flower beds.
- I would then contact my customers and explain these benefits while emphasizing the attractiveness of fresh mulch.
- Typically, I estimated how much mulch I would need by the cubic yard.
- Often times I would order large dump truck loads of mulch to be spread by hand.

- Employees would use large snow shovels to scoop the mulch into their trucks.
- From there they would use wheelbarrows or large plastic containers to distribute the mulch.
- Leveling the mulch with a rake was the final step.
- It was also important to keep this mulch from mounding up around the base of the plants.

Tree Trimming

- Many customers desired to have their trees thinned out and/or pruned once a year.
- Often I would point out the danger of trees touching buildings.
- Even palm trees benefit from a yearly trimming.
- I mostly subcontracted this type of work to professional tree trimming companies.
- Many times I was still able to make a small profit for myself.

Landscaping

- This was one of my best sources of increased profit.
- Because of my existing relationship with my customers, they often hired me when they needed new plants and trees installed.
- We would visit the job site to determine the amount of plants we needed.
- Then we would produce a photo design with landscaping software to present to our customers.
- We would get a price list from our local nursery (which we had a good relationship with).
- From here we would generally double the cost of the plant material to cover labor and overhead expenses.
- This gave us the price we would charge the customer.
- Many lawn maintenance contractors are nervous to take on landscaping jobs.
- I began by sticking to the few plants that I knew grew well in my area.
- As I gained experience, I learned more and more about plant types and how to design beautiful landscapes.
- I would often drop hints to my customers about what landscape ideas might look better when I checked on properties.

- I would usually over bid what my customers asked for in order to make the proposal very stunning.
- Sometimes customers would extend their budgets after seeing how beautiful their landscapes would look with some new plant material.

18. THE CUSTOMER I DIDN'T KNOW I HAD

Customers should be treated well. They were the source of my income. The better I treated my customers, the more money I seemed to make.

However there was one customer that I didn't realize I had. Once I did, things began to change for the better.

That customer was my employees.

That's right, my employees were also a type of customer.

They were the ones coming to work in the blistering heat, pushing their bodies to the limit, and giving all they had each day.

Yet, they were still served by my company. They were human beings with lives, ambitions, goals, and dreams. My employees expected the same level of excellence from me that I expected from them.

This is where the concept of company culture comes in. If I wanted employees who were reliable, had great attitudes, gave their all, and had a sincere desire to advance my company then I needed to give them a good reason to do so.

So I invested in them. I listened to their ideas and helped them to set goals. I fostered a sense of community by providing family based events like picnics and retreats. We gave prizes and incentives. We provided health insurance options above what the law required. We invested in training and personal growth opportunities. We spent time together outside of work. We made sure that there were always opportunities for advancement within the company.

I'll admit that I was not the perfect boss. However, I truly cared about my employees and in return they cared about the company.

19. HOW I HANDLED THE PRESSURE

Owning my own company was one of the greatest experiences of my life. It was also one of the most stressful. Many times I was scared. Everyone looked to me to fix employee problems, mechanical problems, money problems, landscape problems, life problems, and more. I didn't have all the answers all the time.

I will say that it got a little easier over time. Most days were relatively easy and rewarding.

However, some days I felt very inadequate.

It was at these times that I was reminded to go back to the basic principles that I had used for every challenge of life. Everyone has core values. These are the things that drive us.

I established these principles early. If some important decision came up for the company I looked back at my core values. When I was true to my values then the company always seemed to do well - even when I made mistakes.

For me, my core values are closely linked to my faith.

I am a Christian. That didn't mean that I put crosses and Bible verses all over my company marketing materials (although there is nothing wrong with that). However it did mean that my company's values reflected biblical values.

Occasionally this forced me to make some decisions that seemed like they would hurt the company. For example, we didn't work on Sunday's (except one time during a bad hurricane).

Some of my employees questioned my leadership because of these types of decisions. Even my close friends sometimes questioned my choices. That was a tough position to be in.

However, my company grew and I made more money every year I was in business. I trusted God with my company and He took care of the things I couldn't.

20. WHY I WROTE THIS BOOK

After many years of hard work, I received an offer to sell my business for a very large amount of money. Believe it or not the decision was quite difficult. I had poured my life into my business. It wasn't just an organization, it was my life.

I did a lot of thinking, praying, and soul searching. Eventually I was reminded why I started the business in the first place. I did it to make a better life for myself and my family. I made my choice to strike while the iron was hot and sell my lawn maintenance company.

The money I received was incredible. With it, I was able to pursue some life goals that were much bigger than mowing grass. I paid off my home and a few other things as well. I am living my dream and I would not trade that for anything.

Lately I have begun to think about how I got where I am today. In my mind I traveled back to that time just before I began my lawn maintenance business. I was stressed about my job, about my bills, and about my future. I had recently lost my home and had to file bankruptcy. I thought I didn't have any options to make a better life. Most of all, I was scared.

It was then that I realized that there are probably a lot of people out there just like I was. They dream about starting something big but they just need a little push. They need some questions answered. Most of all they need to be inspired.

If you can relate in any way then this book is for you. I know it's a cliché but, if I can do it, anybody can do it.

The biggest mistake you could make would be to let the fear of making mistakes keep you from living your dreams. Yes, there is a risk. Yes, it may not go as planned. Yes, it will be a lot of hard work.

Nonetheless, they say the definition of insanity is doing the same thing over and over again and expecting different results.

Do something different. Do something bold. Do something you have always dreamed of doing.

For me that something was starting my own lawn maintenance business and I have never regretted it.

ABOUT THE AUTHOR

Hello, I'm Mark Koger. For more than 30 years I have worked in the lawn maintenance and landscaping industry. I never went to college. I am not a business expert. I am also not a gifted salesman. However, I have had great success and made a great living mowing grass.

For many years I worked as an employee. I worked hard and did what I was told. After all my effort, I never seemed to get ahead in life. I got brave once and attempted to start an irrigation company of my own. The company ended up failing and I went back to work for someone else. It seemed that my dreams of personal and financial freedom would never come true.

Fast forward to today and everything has changed. I have had great success and made a lot of money. I owned my own lawn maintenance business with more than 30 employees. At its highest point my lawn maintenance company was making well over $1 million a year.

Through struggles and setbacks I was able to unlock many of the secrets to the lawn maintenance industry. Now I want to share what I have learned with others.

I am not a writer (or a reader for that matter). Therefore I intended to write a book that was short and to the point. Some of you may even read through this in one sitting. Either way, I hope that there will be at least a few golden nuggets that you can take and apply to your own business efforts.

This is a book for people who do not know much about the lawn maintenance business. Yet, it will also benefit the seasoned professional. My overall intention is to be helpful. Some of you may finish the book and realize that you still have an important question that was not addressed. If so then please reach out to me on my Facebook page, "Start a Lawn Business" (www.facebook.com/startalawnbusiness).

I will try my best to respond to each question personally.

Made in the USA
Monee, IL
17 March 2022